I0165116

No Easy Answers

A Book of Life-Changing Questions

BARRY MANGIONE

Copyright © 2014 Barry Mangione
All rights reserved.

ISBN: 0692330011
ISBN 13: 9780692330012

This book is dedicated to my wife, Melissa Boyer. Without your unconditional love and support, I would not be the man I am today. Without your inspiration and encouragement, this book would not be possible. I am lucky to have you in my life, and I love you even more than I love buttered coffee in the morning.

PROLOGUE

What is hope?

A few short years ago, I thought I had lost all hope. I filed for divorce and bankruptcy in the same year. I was battling depression and alcoholism. I was suicidal. I saw no future for myself. I saw myself as a failure, and I was certain that the people who loved me were better off without me. I didn't want attention; I just wanted to die. I wasn't going to leave a note or a good-bye video or any kind of explanation. All I knew was that I hurt more than I ever thought possible, and I just wanted it to end.

I had made my peace with God and the universe, and I decided it was time to end my life. I sat in my car in a parking garage in Boston holding a razor blade, ready to slice my neck open and bleed my way into the afterlife. Nothing mattered. My children didn't matter. My parents didn't matter. My family and friends didn't matter. Or so I thought.

Something made me pick up my cell phone and call my friend George. George understood pain. He understood how it felt to want to die. He talked me out of killing myself that night. If it hadn't been for George, I wouldn't be here today.

Hope can be many things to many people. For some, it can be a driving force for change. For others, it can be a paralyzing reason to stay "comfortable" and "safe." It can be motivating and debilitating at the same time. Hope precipitates action but doesn't demand it. I believe hope is the currency of change. It's all about how you spend it, how you invest it, and what you do with it. Keep it locked away in a vault, afraid to cash it in for something great, and you'll be left holding nothing but a handful of hope. Blow it all in the wrong place, and you might never get it back (I can tell you firsthand that having no hope is infinitely worse than having no money). Spend it wisely, do your research, invest your hope in something that brings you even more hope, more potential, and more possibilities, and you'll find yourself on the path to living an extraordinary life. It's not an easy path, and there are no guarantees, but make no mistake about it: hope is essential. You simply can't live without it.

What is hope?

Hope is what made me call George that night.

INTRODUCTION

There are no "secrets" or "laws" or "rules" in these pages. There are a lot of questions and very few answers. If you came here looking for all the solutions to life's problems, you came to the wrong place. If you came here looking for questions to lead you to your own answers, you've come to the right place.

This book is not a substitute for psychotherapy, counseling, addiction treatment programs, or medication. It's not a cure for anything. If you have problems that require medical attention or psychiatric treatment, please get the help you need. There were many books that helped me on my own personal journey, but they weren't the only things that helped me. As you'll find out later in this book, I worked with a therapist, a psychiatrist, a primary care physician, and finally a life coach in order to get to where I am today.

This is not a how-to manual or a step-by-step guide. It's part autobiography, part self-help book. My mission is to set you up to help yourself by telling you my story and by giving you the questions that gave me the knowledge, experience, and tools I needed to go from suicidal to loving life. The questions in these chapters are intended to shift your thinking and open doors to new possibilities.

I won't preach to you. I won't tell you to do exactly what I did or believe everything I say. I'll simply share the experiences and the questions that changed my life and tell you what worked for me. If something in these pages rings true for you, then by all means, apply it to your life. If it doesn't, then don't. Move on to the next chapter, either in this book or in life.

My story is one of recovery, redemption, and reinvention. These stages make up the three main chapters of the book. The questions within the chapters are there to help you navigate your way through the stages, but the questions are only the beginning. What you do with them is up to you. Where you go with them is up to you. Think of them as starting points rather than steps.

You won't win any prizes for answering the questions correctly. In fact, there are no correct answers. That's not the point. As I said before, my mission is to set you up to help yourself. My hope is that this book will change your life.

RECOVERY

Recovery is defined as the return to a normal state of health, mind, or strength. For me, recovery wasn't really about returning to normal. When you find yourself ready to cut your neck open in a parking garage, you have to wonder if your definition of "normal" up to that point was really working. The good news for me was that I realized it wasn't working. Sometimes the biggest problem you can have is not knowing that you have a problem.

Recovery is also defined as the act or process of regaining possession or control of something stolen or lost. Simply put, I had lost control of my life. Think of control as a resource, like gas or food or money. When you're out of gas, you go to a gas station to get more gas. When you're out of food, you go to a supermarket or a restaurant to get more food. When you're out of money, you either go to the bank to get more money or you go to work to make more money. When you're out of control, where do you go? What do you do? That's what I had to figure out: not so much how to get my old life back, but how to gain control of myself in a new way in order to build a new life. I didn't know what that new life would look like, but sure as hell knew I couldn't go back to the old one. So what do you do when you don't know the way? You ask for directions. You ask questions.

WHAT AM I THINKING?

Where did these questions come from? At the risk of sounding crazy, the questions in these chapters came from the voice in my head (don't worry, there's only one voice in my head, and yes, it's my voice). We all have an inner voice. It's the voice that speaks our thoughts to us. Maybe yours is reading this to you right now. Maybe it's what told you to buy this book. I don't know what yours is like, but mine never seems to stop talking, even when I try to meditate (sometimes especially when I try to meditate). My inner voice doesn't believe that less is more. It believes quantity leads to quality. It believes, if it just keeps talking, eventually it'll say something brilliant, so my inner voice says a whole lot of useless, distracting, and occasionally entertaining things before it finally comes up with that rare but precious life-changing idea. I've come to accept that those useless, distracting, and sometimes entertaining thoughts are part of the process that leads to those life-changing epiphanies. The constant chatter is the price I pay for the insightful thoughts that shine through the background noise. I've found that the noise and the chaos are often the fertilizer for clarity and order.

Don't get me wrong. I don't enjoy the constant chatter. I want to be more focused. I try to meditate. Sometimes I even succeed in quieting my mind for a while. There are times when the voice in my head produces some brilliant ideas from that stillness, but, for the most part, my mind prefers to operate more like a shotgun than a laser beam, spraying a large area with ammunition rather than going directly to the center of a bull's-eye with focused energy. So if you've tried to meditate or quiet your mind and you've had a difficult time with it, you're not alone. You're actually in pretty good company.

I struggled with naming what it was that guided me through all the difficult times and desperate moments in my life. At different times I've called it my true self, my soul, the universe, intuition, and even God. For the purpose of this book, I'm going to call it "the voice" or "the inner voice," because everyone has it, regardless of religion, personal beliefs, age, gender, or ethnicity.

One thing I've noticed about the voice is that it's very responsive to the attention and feedback you give it. If you indulge its fantasies, daydreams, and wandering thoughts, it gives you more of the same. However, if you focus more on the insightful questions and search for their answers, you'll find your inner voice asking deeper questions and leading you to a greater understanding of life and of yourself. It might even lead you to moments of that ever-elusive stillness.

"What am I thinking?" is about practical mindfulness. I first started using it in the past tense, looking back at my mistakes and asking, "What *was* I thinking?" Realizing that my thinking was flawed when I made those mistakes showed me the importance of mindfulness, of thinking with purpose in the present moment, so I wouldn't have to ask "What was I thinking?" later. It also works when planning for the future. Whatever project or endeavor you're about to begin, ask yourself what you need to be thinking in order to succeed.

Listen to the voice, but don't obey it blindly. We are not our inner voice. We are the place from which that voice speaks. Our honesty, our experience, our beliefs, our knowledge, and our attitudes shape that voice. If we're not honest with ourselves, our inner voice won't be honest with us. It will betray us, and we will betray ourselves.

Remember, there are no right or wrong answers here. The goal of asking "What am I thinking?" is to become aware of your thoughts and your thought process. We monitor our bodies by taking our temperature when we're sick, or by taking our pulse when we're under physiological stress. How do we monitor our thoughts? By simply asking, "What am I thinking?" in any given situation. Begin to monitor your thoughts. When you're aware of your thoughts and your thought process, you have more control over your life.

AM I BEING HONEST WITH MYSELF?

Sometimes being honest hurts like hell. This is why I lied to myself and to others about so many things for so long. It's also one of the reasons I lost control of my life. Let me introduce the idea of a Control Suck. Going back to the analogy of control as a resource, a Control Suck is something that depletes your supply of control without giving anything valuable in return. Dishonesty is a Control Suck. Lying to yourself and to others uses up energy and depletes the amount of control you have over your life. Having to remember elaborate lies to support other lies takes energy that could otherwise be spent solving problems rather than avoiding them.

After you've become comfortable with asking "What am I thinking?" and you're more aware of your thoughts, ask yourself "Am I being honest with myself?" It's not enough to be aware, to be mindful. Mindfulness without honesty is empty. Being honest is harder than it sounds. I found that out when I entered the world of online dating after my divorce. There's a lot of dishonesty out there in the world. I used to say people were "kidding themselves," but that makes it sound almost cute. The truth is, kidding yourself and lying to yourself are the same thing, and it's harmful no matter what you call it. I didn't appreciate it when someone I met for a first date didn't look anything like her profile picture, and I heard stories from many women who felt the same way about men they met on first dates.

If you're not honest with yourself, then none of the other questions here will lead you toward anything productive or worthwhile. In fact, answering these questions without truly being honest will almost surely lead you to heartache and pain.

How do you know if you're being honest with yourself? There are two sayings about truth that have stood the test of time, because they're both right:

1. The truth hurts.
2. The truth will set you free.

When I started dating again, I decided to be 100 percent honest with people right up front. It sounds crazy, but on a first date, I would come right out and tell my date that I was a bankrupt, divorced alcoholic. I also told them that I was now smarter with money and relationships, and how long I had been sober. I knew that if I entered into a relationship and tried to hide my past, it would eventually catch up with me, and that person wouldn't be able to trust me again. The truth hurt, because I had to own up to my mistakes and lay them out on the table, but it also set me free, because I didn't have to lie about myself or hide who I was. I could be totally comfortable and unafraid of rejection. It hurt because some people judged me for my mistakes, but it also set me free, because far more people appreciated my up-front honesty and were more relaxed and open with me in return. In my opinion, there's no substitute or synonym for honesty. I see the word "transparency" being used when talking about politics and business, but as far as I'm concerned, it's really just a way to avoid using the word "honesty." I hear people talking about "being real" or "getting real" in relationships, but to me it's just another way to avoid saying the word "honesty." Would you rather your politician be transparent with you or be honest with you? Would you rather do business with someone who's transparent or someone who's honest? Would you rather someone "get real" with you or just be honest with you? Personally, I actually feel a physical, visceral reaction to the word "honesty" that I don't feel with any other word. The very word stirs up emotion in me and almost implies a sacred contract.

I'll say it again: for me, there is no substitute or synonym for honesty. As you ask yourself the questions in this book (or any questions you come up with on your own), double-check your answers. Is your voice telling you what you need to hear or just what you want to hear? Does every answer hurt? If so, chances are you're not being completely honest with yourself. The same holds true if every answer feels like it's setting you free. Some of the answers should hurt. Some should set you free. Some of them should do both. If you're only feeling one or the other, go deeper and ask yourself how you arrived at those answers.

HOW DID I GET HERE?

There's a phenomenon I call Taylor Swift Syndrome. My daughters used to be Taylor Swift fans, so consequently, I listened to a lot of her music. If you're not familiar with Taylor Swift, she has an extensive catalog of songs about bad breakups and men who cheated on her and did her wrong. She writes songs about other subjects too, but it seemed to me that she had written a lot of songs about the other person in the relationship always being at fault. I kept waiting for her to release a song called "This Time It Was Me." After my daughters moved on to other musical interests, I stopped listening to Taylor Swift. Maybe she's written that song by now. I honestly don't know.

The point is, for a long time, I suffered from Taylor Swift Syndrome. My problems were always someone else's fault. I always looked for someone else to blame. Whether it was my failed marriage, my bankruptcy, or my alcoholism, I always placed the cause somewhere outside of myself, so I was always waiting for someone else to change or for someone to come along and rescue me. I used to ask "Why me?" all the time. For me, "Why me?" was more of a statement than a question. What I was really saying was "Poor me."

The problem with "Why me?" is it's a Control Suck. It automatically places you in the role of the victim. However, "How did I get here?" places you in a position of control. It forces you to retrace your steps, to look back at what you did and what choices you made. It puts you in the role of the hero at the beginning of a journey, realizing there's a great wrong that must be righted, and you're the only one capable of doing it.

I was stuck in "Why me?" mode for a long time. It was a lot easier to complain and play the victim than it was to even attempt to change my situation. It was much more comfortable to blame the world and my enemies and take whatever they were throwing at me than it was to change myself, my actions, or my choices.

"What was I thinking?" is about retracing your thoughts. "How did I get here?" is about identifying the actions that resulted from those thoughts and analyzing the effects those actions had on your life. Although it's true that there's no "I" in team, you can't spell success or failure without "U."

"How did I get here?" is ultimately about taking responsibility, but before you can take responsibility, you have to identify what you can and can't control.

WHAT DO I HAVE CONTROL OVER?

Some not-so-good news: your thoughts are pretty much all you have control over in this world. Some more not-so-good news: taking control of your thoughts is hard work. The good news: the more control you have over your thoughts, the more control you'll have over your feelings, your choices, your reactions and responses, your habits, and ultimately your life.

The night I quit drinking was the first night that I began to take control of my thoughts. I was separated, living paycheck to paycheck. I had just moved into a typical one-bedroom "divorced guy" apartment after living in my best friend's basement for three months. I had also just suffered a devastating rejection from a relatively short and tumultuous relationship that I foolishly thought was going to be "forever." I felt utterly lost, as if the earth itself had been pulled out from under me. At that time, I had been drinking every day, from the moment I got up in the morning to the moment I passed out drunk at night. My initial reaction to this breakup was to reach for a bottle of vodka and destroy myself, but my inner voice was loud and honest that night, and for a change, I listened to it. The words hurt me and set me free at the same time. The voice said, "If you don't stop drinking tonight, you will die."

I called my friend Mike and asked him to come to my apartment and take every trace of alcohol I had with him. I wasn't going to use a program or go to meetings unless I absolutely had to. I was going to do this on my own. To say it sucked would be the understatement of a lifetime. I stayed alone in my apartment that night and many nights afterward, shaking and crying, hating the process, hating myself, and hating my life, but I kept listening to my inner voice telling me that my drinking problem had nothing to do with alcohol. It had everything to do with my thoughts, my feelings, my choices, my habits, and my reactions. It told me that these were all things that I could control. I couldn't control bad things happening, but I could control how I felt about them and how I reacted to them. I couldn't control what people would say or think about me, but I could control how I felt about myself.

At first, it was terrifying to realize the common factor in my failed relationships, financial hardships, and struggles with addiction was me, but after gaining some clarity and control, it was liberating to realize that the common factor in my victories over depression, addiction, and bankruptcy was also me. No one held a gun to my head and told me to drink. No one threatened to kill my family unless I buried myself in debt. No one ever told me his or her life would be better if I were dead. In the same respect, no one forced me to get sober. No one coerced me into working on myself in therapy. I chose to do all of that myself. I reached what I call a "point of accountability." I got sick of hearing myself bitch and complain about my life every day to my friends and every week in therapy. I realized if I didn't start doing something real during the time between sessions, I was wasting my time and my therapist's time.

Just to be clear, "hitting bottom" and reaching the "point of accountability" are not the same thing. Many people hit bottom, but not everyone reaches the point of accountability. Some people have to hit the bottom many times before they reach the point of accountability. Some never reach it. I was lucky enough to hear the inner voice telling me it was time to stop lying to myself and everyone around me.

It became clear to me that, as hard as I had tried to run from my problems, when I sobered up, they were still right there where I had left them, staring me in the face and breathing down my neck at the same time. They weren't outside of me. They were within me. They weren't separate from me. They were a part of me, so I had to learn to live with myself, and to eventually love myself. I started by paying better attention to my thoughts ("What am I thinking?"). I took one day at a time, sometimes even one minute at a time, listening to the voice saying, "You made it through today. You felt the pain, and you lived. If you were able to do it today, you can get up and do it again tomorrow." Every day was a struggle, but every struggle made me stronger, and I knew there was no turning back.

HOW LONG CAN I KEEP THIS UP?

It doesn't take much effort to live on autopilot. It's seductively easy to coast through life without challenging yourself to grow or to learn. The problem with autopilot is that it's unsustainable. If you want to get somewhere, you're going to have to figure out how to take off and how to land. At some point, problems will come up, and you'll have to take the wheel and steer.

Many times, we overcome one challenge only to find a new and greater challenge waiting for us on the other side. I was pretty proud of myself for figuring out that my drinking problem had nothing to do with alcohol. I was so proud of myself, in fact, that I thought I had it all figured out. I thought I had *all* the answers. I thought I had been drinking because I hated life, or, at least, the life I had created for myself. I was about to find out what I really hated was myself.

After about a year and a half of sobriety, a war broke out inside me. Another failed relationship drew all my shortcomings and failures into sharp focus and opened the door to the idea of suicide. For the first time since I had given up drinking, I wanted to go to a liquor store and get something to numb the pain. At the same time, my inner voice was fighting to remind me how it felt to be drunk: the shame, the physical illness, the lack of control. I remembered hating how it felt and why I had quit. Yes, I had become better at dealing with the pain, but this was a new level of pain. The noise in my head was overwhelming. I stopped listening to the inner voice. I was doing a lot of talking in my head, but I wasn't doing much listening. What was I thinking? I was thinking that I was a failure. I was thinking that I hated myself. I was thinking that life wasn't worth living. I couldn't go back to drinking again, and I couldn't take living with the intense emotional pain I was feeling, so somehow, while completely sober, I decided the only thing left to do was to kill myself. It sounds crazy, but it was the only option I could see at the time. Just as drinking had become unsustainable for me before, life itself had suddenly become unsustainable for me as well.

That was the night I called George. I realize now that just because I stopped consciously listening to my inner voice doesn't mean it stopped talking to me. It never stops talking, and it never stops trying. I'm convinced that my inner voice has a "stealth mode" it goes into, during which it speaks to me on a subliminal level. I believe during those hardest times my inner voice said, "Okay. If flirting with suicide is the only way you're going to realize that you can't keep living this way, let's do this. I'll drive you right to the edge, but I won't let you go all the way. I'll let you break yourself down in order to re-build yourself better and stronger than before, and I'll work behind the scenes. You won't even know hitting bottom was part of the plan until it's over." Like I said before, call it what you will: God, the universe, intuition, the voice...It guided me through those times when I thought I wasn't strong enough to guide myself. I didn't necessarily know where I was going or how my new life would look, but I knew I couldn't keep living my old life. Something had to change. I had been liv-ing from one emotional paycheck to the next, cashing in on happiness from external events, using up that happiness and then crashing into depression when something bad or unex-pected happened. I had to learn the difference between liv-ing one day at a time and living from emotional paycheck to emotional paycheck. The difference was finding happiness within myself and not outside of myself. When you're living from emotional paycheck to emotional paycheck, you're not grateful for what you have in the moment. Instead, you're waiting for whatever's making you happy to be gone, wait-ing for the next bad thing to happen. It's a huge Control Suck. Living from emotional paycheck to emotional paycheck isn't sustainable. Living one day at a time is.

"How long can I keep this up?" is about identifying what's unsustainable in your life. It's about identifying what isn't working and deciding to let it go. It could be an unhealthy hab-it, like smoking or alcohol or drugs. It could be an unhealthy relationship or a criminal lifestyle. It could be your feelings about yourself or about others. It could be an unfulfilling job or career. Whatever it is, it's not always easy to let go. It's not always easy to change. Some people will tell you, "Leap, and the net will appear." What they don't tell you is that the net isn't always suspended high above the ground, waiting to gently catch your fall. Sometimes, it's lying flat on a slab of concrete, waiting for you to break a few bones or get a concussion when you take that leap. The good news is, you can still get up, heal, and move on to something better instead of standing on something you knew was going to crumble under your feet anyway. The even better news is that if you've disengaged your autopilot, you can see the ground coming before you hit it, and maybe even tuck and roll to minimize the damage.

WHAT AM I GRATEFUL FOR?

Things looked pretty bleak for me for a while, but I realize now I was still luckier than most. Things could have been a lot worse. Even at my lowest point, I still had a job. When I was depressed and suicidal, I was lucky enough to have health insurance to cover the cost of prescription meds to help me stabilize my mood. I had a therapist who helped me work through my issues while those meds stabilized my mood. As I was going through bankruptcy, I somehow had enough money to put gas in my car. I lived on ramen noodles and granola bars, but at least I had food. Even though I paid my rent and my bills late every month, I still had a roof over my head. Plenty of people in this world have it way worse than I had it. It was no picnic being suicidal and almost broke, but it helped me appreciate how good things are now. Knowing that other people in the world are worse off than you are is perspective, but perspective and gratitude are not the same. Perspective is intellectual. Gratitude is emotional. It's spiritual. Gratitude isn't just something you experience. It's something you feel. When I was suicidal, I knew I was better off than a lot of other people, but it didn't matter, because I wasn't grateful for all that I had. All I had seemed worthless. Even my life. Something needed to happen to turn my thoughts and perspectives into feelings of gratitude.

The last of my suicidal episodes came right before a Krav Maga class in New York City. It was a weekly class that I hadn't been to in a while, but I went there that night because plans I had made with my daughters fell through at the last minute. I wasn't in control of my thoughts or my feelings at that time. I was genuinely afraid that if I didn't stay busy that night I was going to finally fall far enough into despair to kill myself. If you're not familiar with Krav Maga, it's an Israeli form of martial arts. It's highly effective and very intense. The rigorous physical activity and self-defense drills lifted my mood. I started to feel a little better. My self-preservation instincts had been activated and strengthened. I started to think, "How can I take my life now after I just practiced saving myself from danger for the past hour?" As I walked back to my car after class, I passed a church on West Seventy-Seventh Street where a homeless man was sleeping under a blanket on the front steps. I saw this man who had virtually nothing, and I suddenly became aware of all I had to be grateful for. I didn't forget that I was bankrupt. I didn't forget that I missed seeing my kids every day. My problems didn't magically go away. I just suddenly became aware of all that I did have: two amazing daughters, a job, friends and family who loved me and supported me, an apartment, a car, enough money to buy food (and to make a donation to Coalition for the Homeless, which I did when I got home that night). In that moment, my perspective shifted from what I didn't have to what I did have, and the emotional high I was riding from Krav Maga turned self-preservation into hope. I remember saying out loud to myself, "I'm not done yet. I'm not done yet." I suddenly became aware that I had resources I could use to climb out of the hole I'd dug for myself. I wasn't out of the woods yet, but I wasn't suicidal anymore. I wasn't completely okay yet, but I had faith that eventually I would be.

I realize now that I hadn't lost hope. I had lost sight of my options. I've come to believe that we can never really run out of hope. As I said earlier, I believe hope is the currency of change, but I also see hope as a renewable unlimited energy source, like the sun. We can't always see it, but it's always there. However, just like the sun, hope can burn us if we stay in it too long without moving, and just like the sun, if we go without hope for too long, illness can set in (potentially life-threatening mental or physical illness). Seeing that I had options snapped me out of despair, but feeling grateful for those options is what gave me access to hope once again.

It's no coincidence that I learned the value of gratitude right after a martial arts class. Gratitude is the martial art of emotions. It's self-defense against negative thoughts and feelings. It's armor against despair. Hope stopped me from killing myself the night I called George, but that night on West Seventy-Seventh Street, it was gratitude that made me not want to kill myself anymore. Gratitude gave me something to live for. I still had a long way to go, but I was starting to heal. For the first time, I could see the potential to turn my life around. Since that time, I've made it a daily practice to show gratitude in some way. Every day, either in writing or spoken out loud, I give thanks for at least one thing in my life. Being grateful in and of itself doesn't guarantee happiness, but it's a good place to start. Simply being grateful for my daughters doesn't take care of their needs. Being grateful for life doesn't pay the bills. Being grateful for my wife doesn't mean we don't have to work at our relationship. Being grateful is good. Being grateful and showing your gratitude is better. How do you show gratitude? One way is to live the best life you can possibly live.

REDEMPTION

Redemption is defined as the act of redeeming or atoning for a fault or mistake, or as atonement for guilt. If you've ever had to recover from mistakes or failures, you've no doubt had to deal with your share of guilt. Mistakes come easily. Redemption takes work. Freedom from guilt requires action. There's no Redemption Fairy. You can't just put your mistakes under your pillow at night and wake up to find a shiny new redemption coin in the morning.

Guilt is often what first motivates those of us who've fallen down or made mistakes to get up and make things right. We feel terrible about what we've done, so we want to make ourselves and the person or people we've wronged feel better. Once you've decided to get up and recover, though, as far as I'm concerned, guilt is useless. Let's compare building a new life for ourselves to building a fire. Guilt is good kindling to get the fire started, but it's not a long-term solution to keep the fire going. It's a Control Suck. You can keep a fire going with kindling, but you have to constantly keep throwing more kindling on the fire to keep it alive. Have you ever felt guilty and full of energy at the same time? I haven't. That's because guilt drains you. It takes energy to beat yourself up, and then it takes more energy to heal from that emotional beating. So what's the alternative? If guilt is kindling to get a fire started, what's a big log we can throw on the fire to burn for hours and give us more time, energy, and control over our lives?

Responsibility.

AM I BEING RESPONSIBLE?

I didn't go into debt because I lost my job or because I got sick. I went into debt because of my bad habits. Those habits were the product of the bad choices that I repeated, reinforced, and validated using poor judgment. I never balanced my checkbook, yet I was always shocked and angry whenever I bounced a check. When bill collectors started calling me at all hours of the day and night, I didn't take it seriously. I used to save their numbers in my contacts list. I labeled them Asshole 1, Asshole 2, Asshole 3...I got all the way up to Asshole 33 before it finally stopped being funny.

When I wasn't able to laugh at it anymore, I got angry. I blamed the banks. I blamed the credit card companies. I blamed the government. I attended protests and marches. It felt good to be doing something and to speak out against the injustice of a corrupt financial system, but did all that activism really help me personally? Not much. Blaming others did nothing to make my situation better. It just made me angrier and kept me blind to my own role in creating my personal circumstances. Did the credit card companies give me credit that I didn't deserve? Absolutely. Did I have a responsibility to know better than to overextend myself? Absolutely. Did the banks show poor judgment in giving me a mortgage and a home equity loan that were too big? Of course. Did I show poor judgment in taking those loans instead of tightening my belt and cutting back on expenses? Of course. Is it unfair that big banks got bailed out with taxpayer money after being irresponsible? Yes, it's totally unfair. Did that unfairness absolve me of my personal responsibility to be a good manager of my money for myself and for my family? Hell, no. Going through the process of filing for bankruptcy was one of the best and worst things that could have happened to me. It was hard on me and on my family, but I'm smarter, better, and stronger now for having gone through it. Paying the consequences for my financial mistakes was a responsible act, but that one responsible act didn't automatically make me a responsible person. Quitting drinking was also a responsible act, but that act alone didn't make me a responsible person either. They were both big logs on my fire. They gave me the warmth and the stability I needed to focus my energy on building a better life, but even big logs don't burn forever.

Part of the reason I had so much trouble figuring out how to be responsible was that I still had a bad case of Taylor Swift Syndrome. Luckily, I found treatment before it was too late. I discovered it one day when I looked in the mirror and said, "Maybe it's me." That was the phrase that brought me to the "point of accountability" that I talked about earlier. I'm happy to say that today I'm in remission from Taylor Swift Syndrome. I don't fool myself into believing that I'm completely cured. I know it can come back at any time, but I always know that I can make it go away with those three little words: *maybe it's me.* That's really what the question of "Am I being responsible?" is all about. It's about accepting responsibility for your thoughts and your actions. It's about looking at the recurring patterns in your life and realizing that the common thread running through all your failures and successes is *you.* "Maybe it's me" is about as close to an answer or secret that I'll give you in this book, because it's not really an answer. It's more of a starting point. It doesn't solve any problem in and of itself. It's a catalyst for change. I used to ask myself, "Why do I keep ending up in dysfunctional relationships?" It wasn't until I answered, "Maybe it's me" that things started to change. It wasn't the answer, but it got me asking better questions, like, "What do I keep doing when I'm looking for a partner that keeps attracting people who are bad for me?" I used to ask myself, "Why can't I just get a break?" The catalyst for change was, "Maybe it's me." That answer led me to shift my focus away from thinking the world was out to get me to looking at how I was sabotaging myself.

Like many creative people, I've always been a kid at heart. I never wanted to grow up. I hated the sound of the word "responsibility." I just wanted to write and sing and make music. I equated responsibility with limits and restrictions. I wanted freedom. I wanted independence. The problem is, freedom and independence either don't last very long or don't even happen if they're not balanced with responsibility. Today, I look at responsibility as a foundation and a framework. It's not beautiful, but it doesn't have to be. Without a strong foundation and frame, a beautiful structure like the Sistine Chapel would crumble to the ground. The most beautiful art and architecture in the world would fall apart without a well-designed support system and a strong foundation. That's what responsibility is for me now. I see it as the foundation for my dreams and the framework I use to build those dreams. I can write all the books, music, or lyrics I want, but if I'm not keeping track of my finances or taking good care of myself and my family, the stress resulting from my irresponsibility will override any joy I get from creating art.

I used to think my extreme moods and my addiction were what gave me inspiration. I was afraid that, if I gave up my vices, I wouldn't have anything to write about. The truth is, when I finally did give up my irresponsible behaviors and habits, I was freer. Not only was I was able to write and perform with more focus and creativity, but I was also able to enjoy life on a whole new level. It truly is a balancing act. Responsibility without creativity is lifeless and boring. Creativity without responsibility is dangerous and misleading.

However, unlike the voice, responsibility doesn't exist only in your head. It's not enough to know the right thing to do. You have to actually do it.

WHAT'S THE RIGHT THING TO DO?

This might be the most "loaded" question in the entire book. Many times in my life, I did the wrong thing thinking it was right. Other times, I did what I thought was right only to find out I was very, very wrong. Sometimes the right thing seems wrong, and sometimes the wrong thing seems right at the time (I didn't just pick the title *No Easy Answers* randomly).

I can't tell you what's right or what's wrong for you. You have to decide that for yourself, but I can tell you the strategy I developed to figure out what's the right thing for me. To answer "What's the right thing to do?" I ask myself three questions. You may be wondering how practical it is to use a three-step strategy to make decisions. Sometimes we don't have a lot of time to make difficult or important choices. All I can tell you is that it improves with practice. Like almost anything else, doing the right thing gets easier the more you do it. Try it out in nonpressure situations first. If it works, practice it until it becomes automatic.

The three questions are:

1. How do I feel about myself now?
2. How will I feel about myself after I've done this?
3. How will I feel about myself if I don't do this?

Let's go a little deeper:

1. How do I feel about myself now? Every decision you make leads you somewhere. Before you get where you're going, take a moment first to find out where you are. Call it grounding yourself. Call it finding your center. Whatever you call it, it's the act of being aware of becoming aware of your thoughts and your feelings without judging yourself for them. Just be aware. You don't have to feel completely happy and fulfilled before every decision you make. Sometimes, doing the right thing is so difficult you feel like throwing up. Sure, it's better to act with confidence than to act with fear, but it's important to be okay with your feelings, no matter what they are. You can be uncomfortable or afraid and still make a good decision, as long as you're aware of who you are, what you're thinking, and how you're feeling. Sometimes confidence can be just as dangerous as fear. The key is to own your feelings and to not let them own you. Ownership of your thoughts and your feelings starts with awareness.

2. How will I feel about myself after I've done this? Once you've figured out how you feel about yourself in the present moment, think ahead and imagine you've already done what you've been thinking about doing. How will you feel?

I used to buy things on credit and then feel tremendously guilty afterward. Usually it was a guitar or some other music-related item. Almost immediately after making the purchase, I'd be so racked with guilt that I would either sell it or return it. I couldn't see at the time that getting rid of the item was just as much of a make-me-feel-better-in-the-moment quick fix as getting it in the first place was. It was the same with drinking. I didn't think about how I would feel after doing it. I would just drink and then hate myself for doing it. The drunker I got, the more I hated myself, so I'd have to drink even more. I would drink until I became either so numb or so sick that I didn't care how I felt about myself.

The most extreme examples of not thinking how I would feel after doing something were the times when I was suicidal. When you're thinking about ending your life, you're not really worried about the aftermath, because you won't be there to deal with it. The pain of the moment is so powerful that it's almost impossible to see beyond it. I did, however, get a glimpse into that alternate reality of what might have happened if I had killed myself. A few months after my suicidal episodes, my father was admitted to the hospital with chest pain (my dad had a history of heart problems dating back to the late eighties, and underwent triple bypass surgery in 1990). I was in his hospital room with him when a nurse came in who recognized our last name. She went to high school with my late brother, Alfe, who died in a truck accident in 1998. He was thirty-seven years old. We were all shocked and devastated when it happened. Now, thirteen years later, at the mere mention of Alfe's name, my dad broke down in tears remembering the loss of his son. It dawned on me in that moment that if I had succeeded in killing myself, I would have indirectly killed my dad too. I know, without a doubt, that his heart would not have been able to handle the loss of another child. I saw the past, the present, and the future come together in an instant right there in my dad's hospital room that day. It was my own personal version of *A Christmas Carol* told in the blink of an eye. My dad was discharged a few days later, but I walked out of his hospital room that day with a new appreciation for life and a new sense of responsibility for the second chance I'd been given. "How will I feel about myself after I've done this?" isn't about trying to predict the future. It's about considering the possible outcomes of your actions before acting.

3. How will I feel about myself if I don't do this? After you've figured out how you feel about yourself in the present moment and you've looked ahead to how you'll feel about yourself after you've acted, if you're still not sure what to do, think about how you'll feel if you don't do what you're thinking about doing. If you do nothing, how will your life be different? How will *you* be different? Will you be happy you didn't take that risk, or will you always wonder what would have happened if you had? If you decide to go ahead and do whatever "it" is, will you feel a sense of accomplishment or regret? "How will I feel about myself after I've done this?" is about figuring out whether or not you can live with the consequences or the rewards of your actions. "How will I feel about myself if I don't do this?" is about deciding if you can live with the uncertainty of the future. It's about deciding which unknown you're more comfortable with. I decided I couldn't live with the uncertainty of life as a liar and an alcoholic anymore, but I could live with the uncertainty of just about anything else. You don't always have to see the road ahead of you to know that it's better than the one you're already on.

I mentioned earlier that doing the right thing gets easier with practice. Practice involves doing, not just thinking. Doing involves overcoming fear.

WHAT AM I AFRAID OF?

Fear is my friend. It sounds crazy, but when you find yourself willing to take your own life, you have to overcome your fear of death. Turns out it wasn't fear of death that was holding me back or making me unhappy. It was fear of life. I wasn't afraid of dying; I was afraid of living. Giving up is a lot easier than giving a damn. To me, life is a lot scarier than death. Death is certain. It's going to happen no matter what we do. Life is uncertain. It's the uncertainty of life that scares us, but it doesn't have to. Take a look at of some of the fears that used to dominate my life:

- Fear of losing everything
- Fear of being alone
- Fear of never realizing my dreams
- Fear of rejection

- Fear of other people's opinions
- Fear of failure
- Fear of success

What did all these fears have in common? Uncertainty. There's a "not knowing" involved with every one of them: not knowing how I would pay my bills or feed my kids, not knowing if I would ever find love, not knowing if I would ever do what I really wanted to do in life, not knowing why I wasn't good enough for someone, or if people approved of me or not. The underlying fear in all of these, the fear of uncertainty, was what created story lines for the voice in my head. Instead of being in the moment and dealing with reality, I was constantly thinking of "what ifs" and "should haves." I wasn't focusing on what was happening in the moment. Instead, I was always thinking about what could have happened or should have happened in the past, or what could happen or should happen in the future. I was creating more stress, more anxiety, and more fear for myself. After coming back from the brink of suicide, I had a different relationship with fear. I didn't care what people knew about me anymore. I didn't care what people thought about me anymore. I still had fear, but I decided to treat my fear as a friend and a teacher. Now, when I find myself feeling fear, I ask:

- What is this fear trying to teach me?
- What can I learn from this experience?
- Am I really afraid of whatever this is, or am I afraid of the uncertainty that comes with it?

- If I'm really only afraid of the uncertainty, what's one thing I can I do about it?

I don't believe our fears can be conquered or that they should be conquered. I do, however, believe we can and should face our fears and become intimate friends with them. Fear is the kind of friend that often knows us better than we know ourselves. Fear is the kind of friend that will either get you into trouble or keep you out of it. Fear is a good friend to have, as long as it's not your best friend, or your only friend.

WHAT WOULD I TELL MY BEST FRIEND?

Don't be an askhole. Askholes are people who ask for advice but never follow it. They act like they value your advice, but they completely ignore it. Askholes leave you wondering if they were ever really listening when they asked you for your help.

It was always easier for me to give someone else advice than it was to follow the same advice myself, yet it was infuriating to me when some askhole would ask for my advice and then do whatever he or she was going to do in the first place anyway. Why did it matter to me if he or she followed my advice or not? It mattered because it sucks to watch someone you care about make mistakes that are totally avoidable. Looking back at some of the choices I've made, I guess I used to be an askhole too.

"What advice would you give your best friend?" is about noticing when you're being an askhole with yourself. It's about listening to that inner voice, even when it's telling you what you'd rather not hear. It's about quieting your responses to the inner voice and simply allowing it to speak and to be heard. It's difficult to hear what people are saying to you when all you're thinking about the whole time they're talking to you is what you're going to say back to them. It's also difficult to hear what people are saying to you when you instantly tune them out.

Part of my problem was that when I wasn't being an askhole by ignoring my friends' advice and ignoring my inner voice, I was avoiding being an askhole by stubbornly *not* asking anyone for advice. Like I said earlier, sometimes the biggest problem you can have is not acknowledging that you have a problem. You can't help a friend who's not telling you everything, nor can you help a friend who doesn't want to accept the truth. It goes back to "Am I being honest with myself?" This question is about stepping outside yourself and looking at your life, your choices, and your actions objectively. It's about removing blame and guilt from the equation in order to look at what's happened and then figure out what must be done.

"What would I tell my best friend?" really started out as, "If my best friend came to me with these same problems, what would I say to him? What would I tell him to do?" One of my first responses to this question was, "You're being too hard on yourself. Bad choices don't make you a bad person."

The key to answering this question, "What would I tell my best friend?" lies in finding a balance between ruthless honesty and compassion. The key to finding that balance is to suspend judgment.

WHO AM I TO JUDGE?

Whenever friends would come to me for advice, I wouldn't judge them. It didn't matter to me what they'd done. What mattered was what they would do next. However, when I needed help, I judged myself more harshly than I would ever judge anyone else. What I was going to do next didn't matter nearly as much as punishing myself did. It's hard to help someone when all you're thinking is, "You brought this on yourself. You deserve whatever you get."

I'm not saying judgment in and of itself is bad. We need to be able to judge certain situations and certain people's actions for our own safety and survival, but I'm not talking about judging whether or not your life is in danger. I'm talking about judging people in order to place them into neat little categories that are comfortable for us. It's about placing labels on people, so we can convince ourselves that we understand them without really getting to know them. "Who am I to judge?" is about looking beyond labels and stereotypes, both for others and for yourself.

I'm not perfect. I've certainly done my share of judging others. I've also been judged myself. I've been called a loser, a drunk, and a coward. I've also been called an inspiration, a role model, and a hero. Maybe you've been called one or more of those things too. If you have, who are those people to judge you? If you've called someone else those names, who are you to judge them?

The popular sayings we have about passing judgment don't exactly endorse it:

"Don't judge a book by its cover."
"Don't judge a man unless you've walked a mile in his shoes."
"Judge not, lest ye be judged."

So why do we do it? Why do we put people into neat little boxes with labels on them? Because it's easy. It takes time to get to know a person. It takes effort to discover who someone really is and to find out why they do the things they do, instead of just judging them by their actions. It's just as easy to judge ourselves. When we make mistakes, it's easier to label ourselves as failures than it is to learn from our mistakes and try again. When we succeed, it's easy for our egos to get over-inflated and think we're better than other people.

It's not always about judging people harshly, though. Sometimes we place people on a pedestal, judging them as heroes and role models, only to find out they've hidden some deep, dark secret. Then what do we do? We judge them harshly, at least, until they do something to redeem themselves. Then we judge them as heroes again!

So what's the alternative? Try this strategy:

1. Observe
2. Learn
3. Discern
4. Clarify
5. Accept
6. Reevaluate

1. Observe: That's it. Just observe. Notice people. Notice situations. Observe what people do, what they say, and how they treat you. Observing includes listening. Observe with all your senses, including your "gut feelings."

2. Learn: Take notes (mentally or literally—whatever works for you). Take in everything you've observed and learn from it. Whatever I'm going through—good, bad, or otherwise—I try to remember to ask myself, "What I can learn from this experience?" I try to look at my interactions with others as an opportunity to learn something about them or about myself.

3. Discern: Separate what you see from how you feel about what you see. I know I've said it before, but be honest with yourself. See if how you feel about what you see changes your perception of what's really happening. If I hadn't been able to separate my feelings about my mistakes from my feelings about myself, I may have never given myself a second chance at life. If I hadn't been able to say, "I've failed, but I'm not a failure," I might never have given myself another chance at life.

4. Clarify: Clarify your findings without passing judgment. Does the person you thought of as a role model hold up to your scrutiny and discernment? Are your own actions in line with who you are as a person? Is someone who makes mistakes and questionable choices always a bad person, or does he or she have reasons and a history behind what he or she does? Get some clarity on what you've observed, learned, and discerned.

5. Accept: Accept your findings without the need to be "right." Having to be right all the time will lead you straight down the path to being judgmental, and really, who are you to judge?

6. Reevaluate: Even after observing, learning, discerning, confirming, and accepting, you could still be wrong. You may be right in the moment or at the present time, but your findings could be disproven later. The person you thought so highly of could let you down. The person you thought was such a failure could one day be an inspiration to you. The career path you've chosen could turn out to be unfulfilling. Don't become attached to being right all the time, and don't become attached to labels.

Yes, it's another multistep strategy, but just like the "What's the right thing to do?" strategy, it gets easier and more effective with practice. The sooner you start, the sooner you can become great at it.

WHAT AM I WAITING FOR?

Question: "When's it going to be the right time?"

Answer: The right time is never going to come. Stop waiting for it.

When most people (me included) say they're waiting for the right time, what they're really waiting for is the perfect time, which is also never going to come. I would even argue that the "perfect time" doesn't exist.

I lived most of my life waiting for the right time:

The right time to get married.
The right time to have kids.
The right time to buy a house.
The right time to end my marriage.

The right time to quit drinking.
The right time to ask for help.
The right time to start dating again.
The right time to get married again.
The right time to change careers.
The right time to share my story with the world.

Don't get me wrong, I understand there are times when it's better to act and there are times when it's better to wait. The problem with waiting for the "right time" is that it's a Control Suck. It's not the same as simply taking external factors and circumstances into account when making decisions. It's not the same as weighing all the pros and cons before taking action. Waiting for the right time for me was all about rationalization and procrastination, both of which for me were rooted in fear—fear of change and fear of being wrong.

I used to wait and wait for the right time without ever preparing for it. I thought somehow I'd be instantly ready when all the pieces of my puzzle magically fell into place without any effort from me. I waited for the housing market to keep going up and up, so I could either borrow more money against my equity or sell my house and make a small profit. The right time for that never came. The housing market crashed, and I was left with an underwater mortgage. I waited to quit drinking, thinking I wasn't bad enough to be called an alcoholic. I finally decided I had a problem when I woke up behind the wheel of my car, driving down the wrong side of the road at 3:00 a.m.

After going through so many times waiting for that right time that never came, I decided to take the right time into my own hands. I decided it was time to change careers. I wasn't sure exactly what I wanted to do, but I found myself asking, "How long can I keep this up?" and I didn't want to wait until I reached my breaking point like I had so many other times. I filled out an online application to find a life coach, explaining where I was coming from and where I wanted to go, even though I wasn't completely sure about the "where I wanted to go" part. I just knew I needed a change. Out of the thousands of coaches registered on the coaching website, Steve Borek was the only coach who called me.

It was December 2013, and I told him I wanted to wait until January 1 to begin the coaching program with him. That was going to be my "right time." I planned on New Year's Day being a day of new beginnings. Plus I had some credit card debt that I wanted to pay off before starting the coaching program. Steve listened to me and then challenged me by asking, "Why wait? What's going to be different between now and January first?"

I had no rational answer for this. Being completely honest with myself, I realized nothing was going to be drastically different on January 1. I was still going to be working at the same job. I was still going to be just barely treading water financially. Most, if not all, of my circumstances were going to be about the same. So what was I waiting for?

I was waiting for a guarantee. I was waiting for a sign from the universe. I was waiting for someone to tell me, "Go ahead. Make your move. Everything's going to turn out okay." I used to look for signs like that all the time. I looked for cryptic messages from the universe or from God to tell me I was on the right path, or that it was time to make that move or take that chance. I was waiting for the "all clear" signal from something greater than me. It never came. It still hasn't come. I'm not waiting for it anymore.

You can wait for the right time and hope for a miracle, or you can act now and start building your own miracles. Weighing pros and cons is easy. There's no risk involved with making lists. It might help to see all the pros and cons laid out before you before making a decision or taking a chance, but if you're like I used to be, you can use making lists as a way to stay in your head and out of the world.

Steve was patient with me. I stubbornly stuck with my January 1 start date, but I made a commitment to him and to myself to follow through with it no matter what, and I did start working with him on that day. Three months later, not only did I know where I wanted to go, I knew who I wanted to be. I knew that I wanted to be a writer, a speaker, and a singer. I started writing this book, speaking in public about my personal transformation, and singing and performing regularly at various venues. I even signed a distribution contract for my music with an independent record label based in the UK.

I've placed a lot of emphasis on thinking, but life happens out there in the world as well as inside your head. If you spend too much time thinking about life and not enough time actually living it, you'll be left wondering what happened to you and where your life went. "What am I waiting for?" is about figuring out what's stopping you from doing what you want to do, being who you want to be, and living your dreams.

Here's another one of the few times I'll give you an answer to one of the questions, but it's actually another question disguised as an answer.

Question: "What am I waiting for?"
Answer: IDK

No, IDK doesn't stand for I Don't Know. In this case, it stands for Identify Dream Killers. Dream killers are thoughts that limit you and keep you from realizing your true potential. Identify them, and you'll find out what's holding you back from doing what you want to do and being who you want to be. Examples of dream killers are:

I'm too old.
I'm too young.
I don't have enough experience.
I could never make a living doing what I love.
I'm not talented enough.
I can't change.
I have to do what people expect of me.

Most dream killers are rooted in the past. Don't judge yourself by your past. Instead, use the six-step strategy I outlined, placing a special emphasis on learning when looking at your past. There are plenty more dream killers than what I listed here, but the point is, if you want to move from redemption to reinvention, you have to get out of your own way. If you want to move from getting your life back to creating a new life, you have to remove the roadblocks and barriers that you've put in place. There will be plenty of real roadblocks and barriers that come from outside of you. Why add to them?

Instead of putting roadblocks and barriers in your way, why not build a bridge between the present and the future? Why not build a bridge between who you are now and who you want to be? Judgment is a bridge that will carry you back to the past. Forgiveness is a bridge that gives you access to your future. Judging yourself for what you've done in the past will keep you in the past. If you've made mistakes, own up to them, acknowledge them, repair the damage if you can, and most importantly, forgive yourself and move on. Forgiving yourself doesn't mean excusing yourself for making those mistakes. It also doesn't mean allowing others to hurt you again. When I was finally able to forgive myself for my mistakes, I had the freedom to either correct them or make amends for them. When I was able to forgive others for the hurt they had caused me, I didn't have to carry the weight of hatred, anger, and resentment on my shoulders anymore. I felt free. It didn't mean that what they did to me was okay, it just meant that I wasn't going to let those thoughts and feelings use up so much of my energy.

I realized that every moment I spent being angry at someone was a moment that I could spend being happy or following my dreams. Time isn't a resource like money. When you use it up, you can't just go make more. I used to say, "There aren't enough hours in the day." I don't say that anymore, because no matter how much I try to change it, there will always be the same number of hours in a day. If I feel like there aren't enough, it's because I'm not making the most of those hours. Learning forgiveness taught me the value of making the most of my time. You can't get all the time you spend waiting for the "right time" back, so why keep waiting? Why not decide when the right time is, commit to it, and use whatever time you have before it to prepare yourself to make the most of it when it comes? Procrastination is a Control Suck. Judgment is a Control Suck. If you're spending your time procrastinating and judging instead of living the life of your dreams, ask yourself, "What am I waiting for?" If that doesn't work, ask yourself, "How is this helping me?"

REINVENTION

To reinvent is to invent again or anew—to remake in a different form. If you have it in you to imagine a new you, you have it in yourself to become that new you, but imagination alone isn't enough. Here's what my tai chi instructor says about imagination: "People say imagination becomes reality. I disagree. Imagination becomes daydreams. Visualization becomes reality."

What he's saying is that when it comes to producing results and making things happen, imagination is good, but visualization is better. Visualization is imagination with intent and purpose. Reinvention doesn't happen on its own. It requires imagination, intent, purpose, dedication, determination, and hard work.

WHAT DO I DO NOW?

So you've recovered and redeemed yourself. What now? For me, redemption wasn't enough, nor was it the end of my journey. I didn't save myself from death at my own hands to live an ordinary life. I didn't want to just "not hurt" anymore. I wanted to be happy and fulfilled. I wanted to live *with* purpose and *on* purpose. I couldn't just coast by on autopilot anymore. It was time to create a new life, but how the hell was I going to do that?

From my coaching sessions with Steve, I knew who I wanted to be: a writer, a speaker, and a singer. So the answer to "What do I do now?" should have been easy, right? All I had to do was start writing, speaking, and singing, and then everything else would just magically fall into place for me, right?

Wrong.

Imagination had never been a problem for me, and I was now starting to enjoy the hard work of putting myself out there, writing, speaking, and singing. I wasn't discouraged by rejection anymore. Through the process of getting sober and becoming friends with fear, I had the dedication and determination to overcome obstacles and adversity. What was missing from my efforts was intent and purpose. Although it's true you don't always have to know where you're going or who you want to be in order to make a change, that time does eventually come, and it had come for me.

I knew who I wanted to be. I knew what I wanted to do. I knew where I wanted to go with my career and my life. I had the who, what, and where. I needed to figure out the how, the why, and the when. I didn't want to spend the rest of my life working hard only to look back and ask, "What was it all for?"

I had been working hard, but I'd been working without a plan, without a vision, and without goals. I had been afraid of setting goals before because I was afraid of not achieving them, but now it was time to get over that fear. My inner voice said, "Guess what? You've already failed! You've failed many times in your life, and you're still here. You're better and smarter now, because you've learned from your failures. Use what you've learned. Start setting goals again. If you fail, look at why you failed and set your next goals accordingly. If you achieve them, look at how you did it and use that knowledge and experience to reach higher next time. The goal itself is important, but how you get there is just as important, if not more important."

HOW DO I GET THERE?

Ask for directions.

I used to look at other people who were "better off" than me and think, "Must be nice," which for me was really a shortened version of "It must be nice to not have to deal with all the hardships and obstacles that I've had to overcome in life. That person must have it way easier than I do, because if he had to deal with what I have to deal with, he'd probably curl up in the fetal position and cry his eyes out. If I got all the same lucky breaks he got, I'd be right where he is too, but unlike him, I got dealt a crappy hand, so I'll just sit over here in the 'Sucks to Be Me' corner."

Now when I find myself wanting to say "Must be nice," I stop myself and ask, "How did they get there? How did they do that?" Sometimes, if I feel comfortable enough with that person, I'll ask him or her personally how he or she got there and how he or she did it. Try it. You may be surprised to find out that some of those people overcame tremendous obstacles to get where they are. They may have valuable knowledge and experience that could help you on your journey.

I'm not the first person to ever reinvent himself. In order to be a writer, speaker, and singer, I had to do some research to find out how other people had done it before me. I wanted to find out how they got "there" and what they had to do every day to stay "there." I read books and blogs. I listened to podcasts. I watched documentaries and videos. I talked to people who were already doing what I wanted to do.

I found out that the what, the where, and the how were flexible, meaning when you set out to reinvent yourself, you may discover that what you want to do, where you want to go, and how you get there can change as you learn more about yourself on your journey. It's important to be open to possibilities and opportunities and to adapt to changes. Rarely does everything go exactly according to plan. After all, the only things you can truly control are your thoughts, right?

The *who* and the *why* were constant and often one and the same. Everyone knew who he or she wanted to be and why. "Why do I do what I do? I have to. It's who I am." Once again, the only thing you can truly control is your thoughts. Once you know who you are and know your purpose (your "why"), there's no turning back.

The "when" is what I call a "moving constant." Some people set a deadline for when they wanted to achieve their goals and stuck to it no matter what. Others set specific goals and times, but when they didn't reach those goals at the times they had planned, they adjusted their timeline and kept working on those goals until they achieved them. The lesson I took away from this was that if you don't set a time, you're wasting time. Not setting a date or a deadline for your goals is a Control Suck. It's an open invitation for excuses, procrastination, and rationalization. If you're working on reinventing yourself, set goals, pick a date, and start working on them today.

But don't do it alone!

WHO'S WITH ME?

One of the most courageous things a person can do is to ask for help and accept help when someone offers it to them. No matter where "there" is for you, you can't get there on your own.

The summer after I left my wife and kids, I didn't know what to do with myself. When I wasn't looking for answers in liquor stores, I looked for help and support from my friends. There's nothing quite like adversity to show you who your real friends are. Even through my drunken and depressed fog, it was easy to see who was "with me" and who wasn't. Looking back at the person I was at that time, though, I'm not sure if I would have been friends with me during those dark times.

My friend Domenic was one of those friends who was definitely "with me" during that time. Besides being a good coworker, Domenic was just a great guy to know. He was both a man's man and a ladies' man—a PhD neuropsychologist and a veteran of a few divorces. I asked him how the hell he got through the loneliness, the despair, and the separation from his kids. He told me two things. His first piece of advice was, "Anybody who's not supporting you one hundred percent... Cut 'em loose. You don't need 'em." His second piece of advice was simply "Get laid."

I was way too depressed to even think about getting laid, but I didn't want to be a complete askhole, so I followed through on his advice regarding friendship. I stopped looking for help where I wasn't going to get it. I gave time and energy to relationships and people that gave me time and energy in return. It worked. Slowly, I started to turn things around in both my inner and outer worlds. I found it was better to have a small group of close, reliable, supportive friends than it was to have a large group of friends who weren't going to be there when you needed them. It wasn't about punishing people or getting back at them for not being "with me." It was about re-alizing that my time and my attention were valuable resources and I should spend them wisely.

Success doesn't happen in a vacuum. Neither does failure. If you want to succeed in anything, you need people around you who will help you succeed: people whose talents complement yours, people who know things that you don't, people who have skills that you don't have. You also need to be aware of and stay away from people who will drag you down, hold you back, and discourage you.

How do you attract supportive people to you? How do you create a great team of people to help you achieve your goals? Be the kind of person someone else would want on his or her team. If you want to be successful, help someone else be successful. Help someone else achieve his or her goals. Throughout my research on recovery, redemption, and re-invention, this was a universal principle. If you want to go somewhere, help someone else get where he or she is going. If you want to get something, offer something. If you want someone to be there for you, be there for someone.

HOW CAN I HELP?

If we're not here to help each other, then why are we here?

This is the question that motivated me to share my story. I had to believe that I went through all I went through for a reason, and that reason was to help others going through the same experiences. Why keep what I'd learned to myself if someone else could benefit from it?

When it comes to reinventing yourself, you're not alone. People you know will be affected by the change in you. The world around you and the world at large will also be affected by the change in you. Part of reinventing yourself is asking how you can be of service to others. How will the new you change the world? When I say change the world, I don't mean you have to be the next Gandhi or Martin Luther King. Changing the world doesn't mean everyone in the world has to know your name. You can change the world by changing one person's life in a positive way. It's easy to get wrapped up in the "self" part of reinventing yourself, but the new you is still going to be a part of a local and a global community (unless you decide to reinvent yourself as a hermit).

"How can I help?" is about giving back. I struggled with the idea of giving back being part of reinvention. I worked for several decades helping others as a physical therapist. I felt like I'd given all I could give, and I figured it was time to help myself for a change. The idea of helping others didn't seem like reinvention to me, even though it was a common thread running through all the information I researched. As I continued to work on myself, however, it became clear that it didn't matter how much I'd changed if I didn't put those changes to good use in the world.

Being of service doesn't have to mean volunteering twelve hours a day or traveling to third world countries to save the world from poverty and disease. Being of service can be as simple as being a good friend, a good parent, a good spouse, or a good coworker. Simply being a better "you" is an act of service, because being the best you can be and doing the best you can do makes everyone's life easier. When people know they can count on you as a friend, you're being of service. When coworkers know they can count on you, you're being of service.

When I started looking at helping others as an act of service rather than an act of self-sacrifice, I was finally able to help others without burning myself out. I also had a greater appreciation for the little things people did for me every day. I went from starting out with small acts of service on a personal level to working with volunteer groups and fundraising for charities.

"Who's with me?" is about finding and assembling your team. "How can I help?" is about being a valuable team player. There's no "I" in team, but success and failure both have "U" in them. Who "U" are and what "U" do, big or small, makes a difference for yourself and for others.

WHAT'S THE POINT?

Who you are and what you do makes a difference in the world. "What's the point?" is about finding the reason why we do what we do. Have you ever had a conversation with someone who just rambles on and on without having a point? Was it draining? Did you feel like your time was wasted? Imagine for a second that your inner voice is the voice of your life speaking to you, asking you, "What's the point? Why are we here? What's the purpose behind all of this?"

What would your answer be?

I found my purpose doing volunteer work in the rural Appalachia region of America with Appalachia Service Project (asphome.org). I was an adult team leader for a group of ten teenagers. Our job was to build a retaining wall behind a family's home to keep water runoff and mudslides from the mountain behind their house from ruining their home. We had five days to complete the job, which involved moving more than twenty-five tons of rock by hand up a hill behind their house and then placing them in wire structures called Gabion baskets. It was hard work, but for five days I woke up early, and I woke up with a clear sense of purpose. We encountered adversity when we ran out of rocks with only half a basket left to fill at the end of the third day. We only needed about two more tons, but the quarry wouldn't deliver a "small load" that size. Every one of the young people on my team had worked so hard and wanted to finish this job, so we came up with an idea. We asked the homeowner where we could find more rocks. She told us we could use any rocks lying around the yard. She also told us there was a creek across the street where we would find more rocks. We carried rocks from around the yard and from across the street and finished the job on the fifth day. It was incredibly satisfying to know that we had helped the family by making their home safer and to know that we had achieved what we set out to do.

At first, I thought my positive energy and mood every morning was because my purpose was pretty simple: carry rocks up a hill and build a wall. Building the wall wasn't my purpose, though. My purpose there was to be a leader. I hadn't really thought of myself as much of a leader up until that point. For many years, it had been enough of a challenge just to lead myself out of despair and depression. Yes, I enjoyed the physical work, but what was truly uplifting and inspiring was the opportunity to lead people and be a role model for them. I realized on the long drive home from that trip that I had been a leader in other areas of my life without knowing it: I was a lead singer. I was a lead guitarist. I was always the person to whom friends would come for advice. I was always the person people at work sought out when there was an emergency. For the first time, however, in Appalachia, being a leader felt right. It felt like I was doing what I was supposed to be doing with my life. I used to think a leader had to be authoritarian and controlling. I realized that the best way to lead is by example. This became more and more clear to me as people started noticing my transformation from being depressed, addicted, and suicidal to being motivated, focused, and happy. Today, people come up to me and ask, "How do I get where you are? How did you do it?"

We're all in this together. Every person you meet has something to teach you. Every life experience is a lesson waiting to be learned. If we don't help each other, what's the point?

HOW DO I KNOW?

How do I know if what I'm doing is working?
    How do I know if I can trust my inner voice?
    How do I know if I can trust myself?
    How do I know if I'm going in the right direction?
    How do I know I'm not going to go back to my old ways?
    How do I know if I'm making the right decision?

"How do I know?" is the voice of fear disguised as the voice of reason. It's not just a question you ask yourself. It's questioning yourself. It's questioning everything you've done and everything you're about to do.

I can't give you the answer to "How do I know?" but I can give you my strategy for answering it. Not surprisingly, it involves asking yourself four more questions:

1. Have I done everything I possibly can?
2. Am I balanced or off-balance?
3. What have I got to lose?
4. What have I got to gain?

1. Have I done everything I possibly can? If you're unsure about what you're about to do, ask yourself if you've done everything you can in order to set yourself up for success. If you have, move on to the next question. If you haven't, go back and do more to prepare yourself for what you're about to do, but remember to be honest with yourself. Be honest about what you need to do. Don't let preparation turn into procrastination.

2. Am I balanced or off-balance? Being balanced doesn't mean you're as steady as a rock and 100 percent sure of every move you make all the time. It just means the world outside you doesn't dictate who you are inside. Life can sometimes be unpredictable. Sometimes, asking "Have I done everything I possibly can?" isn't an option because you don't have time. That's why it's important to have balance. Balance is a state of relaxed readiness. It means being ready for nothing to happen or for anything to happen. Looking back at the decisions I made and the things I did when I was drinking and when I was suicidal, I realize I was incredibly off-balance but didn't see it at the time. How did I become more balanced? How did I become more relaxed and ready? I talked to my fear. I listened to my inner voice. I asked and answered questions, I tried new things, and I ventured outside my comfort zone. I tried until I got things right, and I tried until I didn't have to try anymore. When "trying" became "doing," "not knowing" turned into "knowing."

3. What have I got to lose? You're either comfortable with not knowing or you're not. In my experience, if I'm asking "How do I know?" then I'm not comfortable. Whether it's applying for a new job, asking someone out on a date, starting your own business, or chasing a dream, ask yourself "What have I got to lose?"

4. What have I got to gain? Again, you're either comfortable with not knowing or you're not. How will you know if you don't try? At the very least, what you stand to gain is knowing the answer to "How do I know?"

I've talked a lot about my inner voice, but there are two other voices that I haven't mentioned. That's because they don't say much. They pretty much just nod their heads "yes" or shake their heads "no." I recommend you consult these other voices if you're still having difficulty overcoming "How do I know?"

The first is your heart. Listen to your heart. When your heart and your head agree, you're in good shape. When your heart and head are at odds with each other, take more time and ask more questions to figure things out.

The second is your gut. What does your gut tell you? When your head and your gut agree, you're in good shape. When your head and your gut are at odds with each other, you'll know it. If that's the case, take more time to figure things out.

If your head, your heart, and your gut are all on the same page, you'll know it. You will feel balanced, relaxed, and confident. You won't worry about what's coming next, because you'll know you can handle whatever comes your way. You won't pat yourself on the back too much for your achievements, because you'll know you have more work to do and more goals to achieve. The best example of this for me was falling in love with my wife, Melissa. After our second date, I knew beyond a doubt that she was the one for me and that we were perfect for each other. My head, my heart, and my gut all agreed. Before I met Melissa, I had never had all three voices on the same page. There was always, at least, a hint of uncertainty in my head or my heart or my gut, but when we got together, I didn't have to worry about when to call her or when to text her. I didn't have to think about the right things to say; I just said them naturally. I didn't think I would ever get married again after my divorce, but when I met her, I wasn't afraid anymore. I knew we would be happy together.

In a world of no easy answers, sometimes the answer to "How do I know?" is simply "I just know."

EPILOGUE

My tai chi instructor has a saying about practicing tai chi: "We strive for perfection, knowing we'll never reach it."

None of us will ever be perfect, but that doesn't mean we stop practicing. It doesn't mean we stop trying to live the best life we can live and be the best person we can be. I encourage you to live the best life you can. I encourage you to be the best "you" you can be.

"Encourage" means to inspire with courage, spirit, or confidence. I hope this book has encouraged you in some way. If it has, please let me know at barrymangione.com.

THANK YOU

I would like to thank everyone who helped make this book possible:

My backers on Kickstarter: Delia Stanley, Anthony Cardno, Leeann Coffin, Rikki Boyer Hayes, Mary Stark, Chris Daniele, Gregry Gilroy, David Henningsen, Angelo Escobar, Jack D'Orio, Ilaine and George Wissing, Paul Stein, Natasha Hadley, Jennifer Sarah Blakeslee, Chris Dudding, Patrick Kearney, Stephen Lackey, Jim Nardone, Brittany Finch Prior, Tom Capasso, Ashley Linson, Steve Borek, Stacy Lanyon, David Soska, Aimee Taft, Christi Widerstrom, Tony Mazzarella, Hope Caulfield, Sandy Scanlon Lucke, Karen Eiler, Donna Lauer, Ro Carlson, Sam Daley, InfinityLtd, Diana Vukel, Clay Pierce, Chris D'Orio, Wayne Antal, Hunter Martin, Sdhari Cason-Payano, Darrell Long, Michelle, Brandon Eaton (aka Boss B), Tim Maitland, Maggy Donaghy Duffy, Elena Swan, Carolyn Doyle, Provvidenza Guastella-Varuolo, and Michael Boyer. Honorable mention to Michele Sarti Vukovich for her post-Kickstarter support.

Special thanks: to my sister-in-law, Tara Fairbrother, for her belief in me and in my writing, and for being an example of how to balance a youthful spirit with an old soul; to George Haslin, for being there when I needed him the most and for saving my life that with his words and his heart that night in Boston; to Marie Mascia-Mancl, for saving my life again, and for threatening to end our friendship if I didn't start saving myself; to my nonbiological sister, Diana Vukel, for her love, support, and spiritual guidance; to Darrell Long for giving me a place to stay when I needed one; to Natasha Hadley for always being there for me, and to Nelson Rivera, for the phone call back in June 2012 that gave me the courage to eventually write this book. Additional thanks to anyone I've forgotten.

Photography: cover photo by Jennifer Sarah Blakeslee (jennifersarahblakeslee.com); author photo by Denise Cregier (denisecregier.net).

A portion of the profits from this book will be donated to Appalachia Service Project to support the work they do rebuilding and repairing homes. I will also continue to volunteer with my local A.S.P. Chapter. To find out more about A.S.P., go to asphome.org.

www.ingramcontent.com/pod-product-compliance
Lightning Source LLC
Chambersburg PA
CBHW020557030426
42337CB00013B/1129